NIGHT FISHING

NIGHT FISHING

A Woman's Dream Journal

Katherine Metcalf Nelson

GIBBS·SMITH
P
PUBLISHER

Salt Lake City, Utah

Art historian, writer, editor, and Master Gardener, Katherine Metcalf Nelson has taught at Westminster College, Mississippi State College, California College of Arts and Crafts, and the University of California. She has written numerous articles and is the author of Apricot Eggs, *an autobiographical fish tale. In addition, Nelson has been an editor for* Utah Holiday *and* ARTnews. *She now lives in Seattle, Washington, where she works in a nursery, refining her skills as a Master Gardener.*

First Edition

99 98 97 3 2 1

This is a Peregrine Smith Book, published by
Gibbs Smith, Publisher
P.O. Box 667
Layton, UT 84041

Designed by Kinde Nebeker
Edited by Gail Yngve
Apricot Eggs, reprinted compliments of the Phillips Gallery

Printed and bound in Asia

Library of Congress Cataloging-in-Publication Data
Nelson, Katherine Metcalf, 1940-
   Night fishing : a woman's dream jounal / Katherine Metcalf Nelson.—1st ed.
   ISBN 0-87905-790-4
   1. Dreams. 2. Healing. 3. Dreams in art. 4. Nelson, Katherine Metcalf, 1940—
Diaries. 5. Nelson, Katherine Metcalf, 1940—Health. I. Title.
BF 1099.S76N45 1997
154.6'3'092—dc20   96-40966
                          CIP

Woman-fish
in an oval dish
on the altar
of the Holy Fisherman
in the middle
of the Holy See.

Eight years
it took
to unhook
anger and affection,
bleeding and birth,
wounds and wings.

Eight years

TABLE OF CONTENTS

Steel Compartments	6	Ax in My Back	55
Vision of Alma	9	Wedding Basket	56
Magi and Animals	10	Explosion	59
Fish Birth	13	Flying Fish and Lotus I	61
Artspace	14	II	62
Fishing with a Hand-Tied Fly	17	Half a Fish	65
Red Rock Spirit	18	Inside My Molar	66
Fishbowl	21	Ancient Book of Days	69
A Landscaping Job	22	Essence	70
Butterfly in a Globe	25	Sophia	73
New Lines from an Old Tree	26	Pool of Truth	74
Frozen River	29	Return to the Tree	77
Bleached Skull	30	Tree-Woman	78
High and Low Fantasy	33	Ascent of the Dolphin	81
Plumber's Helper	34	Clinging Crab	82
Road within a Circle	37	Star Canoe	85
Artichoke Plate	38	Tattoo of Transformation	86
Magic Finger	41	Medicine Bag	89
Nevada and Colorado	42	Three Women in One	90
Amaretto	44	Diamond Pattern	93
Brass Ring	47	Self-Portrait Done by Hand	94
Bathsheba at Belvedere	48	Roman Substructure	97
The Great Wave	51	Ursa Major	98
T'ai Chi Circle	52	My Grandmother's Ring	101

Fountain	102
My Egypt	105
Rainbow Pot	106
Old Testament or New?	109
Grand Hotel	110
Public Events Versus Snakes From India	113
On the Move	114
Perfect Tree	117
Polaris Compass	118
Bottom of the Pond	121
A View Inside	122
Espresso	125
Sleep Writing and Star Watching	126
Passport to Spring	129
Open Book	130
From Art Class to St. Peter's	133
Between Sun and Moon	134
Hydra Beads	137
Sunshield	138
Word Quilt	141
Paris-London Line	142
Fish Remains	145
Your Own Night Fishing	147-160

*For dream catchers who
fish in the dark.*

Introduction

A P R I C O T   E G G S

My story is a fish story, forty-four years of swimming around from minnowhood through motherhood. My father taught me to fish in a green dory in San Francisco Bay and in High Sierra streams. "Be patient with yourself," he said, "and look carefully into the water. If you are quiet like a fish, you'll catch one." I did.

There were many catches and releases. Some days I felt sorry for a salmon in the bottom of the boat. Some days I pushed baby perch out of their mother's belly, hoping I was returning someone to the sea. Once in a while I was triumphant having landed a big golden or brook trout for dinner by a campfire.

As a child my best days were water days, watching changes in a tideline or stream current. Being without thinking—dreaming, floating, and looking beneath the surface. Fish taught me about birth, about death, about struggle and surrender, about the fine line between laughter and tears, between give and take.

I felt uneasy when I took and I didn't need to, but I kept on fishing. I taught my husband and my children how to fish, and so we came to the banks of the Provo in September. Julie and I went downstream; my son, John, and his father upstream. Cows, sheep, spinner fishermen, and a couple of kiddie-filled families wandered in and out of the water, noisily rolling rocks underfoot. No luck all morning so we returned to the pasture by the bridge for lunch, ate our sandwiches, and watched grasshoppers bursting forth in all directions.

We talked about the river. How beautiful it must have been before the Army Corps of Engineers bulldozed it for flood control, before an angry farmer dumped in Clorox, killing nearly all the fish on the south fork.

Definitely, this was a bad fishing day, but we went back to the deep pool by the old wooden bridge, the womb of the river that received everything from garlic cheese and flashing spinners to car fenders and an occasional aluminum can. Julie hooked a small cutthroat, and was nearly in tears when it got away. John stood knee-deep in the lower end of the pool, putting out yards of yellow line and snarling his leader and his temper. I sat on the bank, half-heartedly giving fly-casting lessons, and thinking, *poor, empty, half-dead river.*

My husband, Jim, crossed the bridge and went upstream to where a feeder creek

flowed into the main channel. Before long, he returned, proudly holding a heavy German brown that bent in his net. "Should we keep it?" he asked. His voice was excited and uncertain—that thin line between give or take. The magnificence of the fish and the poverty of the river weighed against each other.

"Take it," I answered. "The river is dying anyway. We can cut it open and find out what the fish are eating." My verdict made me queasy, but I pushed down my feelings. "Jim, let me get a picture," I said. "That's some catch!" I fiddled with the camera while the trout wiggled as he held it by its gills in midair. It dropped in the sand, was washed and rehung in focus for Kodak.

As I clicked the shutter, I thought, *How strange. I never take pictures of fish.*

Jim went to the water to clean it. His knife slit its underside. Its head thrashed hard a couple of times and was still. He reached inside to take out guts, gills, and fins, and saw a belly full of apricot eggs. "Kate, we've made a terrible mistake. She is full of roe." I was stunned. I thought trout spawned in spring, not fall. If they were spawning, why was the river even open for fishing?

Jim tossed her guts into the current and placed her eggs in the shallows. We watched them settle in two large clumps between the rocks. Then he wrapped her and put her in the cooler.

I sat by the water, thinking, *I should not have decided for that fish. I didn't even catch her.*

That night we poached her for dinner. Jim ate most of her. Julie and I didn't eat much. Lemon helped, but she was hard to swallow.

I couldn't sleep thinking how abundantly full of life she had been and how near to birthing. I began to weep. We were the same age in our life cycle. Many seasons of egg-carrying upstream and down, not too many egg-bearing seasons left. How round and shiny and orange they were. Thank God, Jim had returned them to the river. At least that put some giving into the taking.

She brought me to tears again when I retold her story to a woman who knows me well. "Katie," she said, "you've known that fish all of your life. And those apricot eggs, they are your dreams."

My friend is right. I was born in September, cut out of my mother's womb by caesarean section one month early. In midlife I was unexpectedly opened up for cancer

and skillfully put back into the stream with a fishhook scar down the right side of my nose. That's when I began to draw my dreams.

I told my friend about the magic fish I had met as a child. I was rowing in a green boat when she leaped into the air in front of me. Balancing on her tail, her brown eyes meeting mine, she said, "Your time will come. You'll see." We both burst out laughing, and she disappeared.

But that was "once upon a time" when I lived by the sea. I forgot about the fish in the midst of growing up, marrying, birthing, and caring. It wasn't until years later when I moved to the Utah desert that she returned, and I began to see. As I changed, so did she.

A baroque goldfish with an injured tail who flopped out of her bowl to become my daughter.

A mother walrus who rose from the ocean to protect her children on shore.

A dead steelhead whose right half was eaten to the bone.

A salmon and her mate treading water above a giant red egg.

A silver carp that my son pulled out of Lake Powell.

A smiling cutthroat who swam to the bank to talk, was frightened by fishermen, and slid back into the stream as a spotted seal.

A rainbow trout trapped in a half-frozen pothole in a parking lot off Main Street.

A paper whale that spouted forth at *The New Yorker*, floating in a sea of green velvet and white marble.

A pregnant perch pulled up from the bottom of San Francisco Bay on piano wire and dragged in across debris, tidal foam, and flotsam.

A dolphin who ascended from the deep to become the cover of a book.

Best of all was the flying trout with wise eyes and rainbow wings that I brought out of a pool with my hands, rested on a rock beside me, and returned to the water. Whenever I needed to go down into myself and look around, the fish was there.

In gratitude to her, I call my diary Night Fishing. On the surface it is a chronology of dreams. Beneath dreams are pictures. Beneath pictures is a poem that I retrieved when I returned to restring my pearls.

My night journey began on my thirty-seventh birthday in a dream that recurred three times until I wrote it down and sent it to a friend in California. Her response gave me encouraging advice: "In spite of your fear, your fascination to meet the event signals your openness to this mysterious dimension. The unconscious speaks a curious language of its own. I hope you will have a long conversation with yours."

So my conversation begins . . .

STEEL COMPARTMENTS

A glistening metallic chamber fills a barren desert. *Cautiously I approach.* Immense and cold and *tightly shut.* How gray the landscape and the evening light.

Fear and admiration. I scrutinize the smoothness of its silvery reflecting surfaces. Subtle riveting of bolts. Exquisitely fitted compartments. Rounded corners, worn like edges of an antique table. A complex order of shining intellect made with patient craft. An old storage box on the edge of an Aquarian age.

Cold from a distance. Warm up close. Heat from inside burns red in my palms as I scan with open hands. Fingers pass over steel that feels like sunlight coming through glass. Hard, rectangular shapes become smoothly rounded curves, hypnotic to touch. An impenetrable block dissolves into a translucent veil, shielding a radiance of colored light.

Fright becomes fascination as I search to see inside.

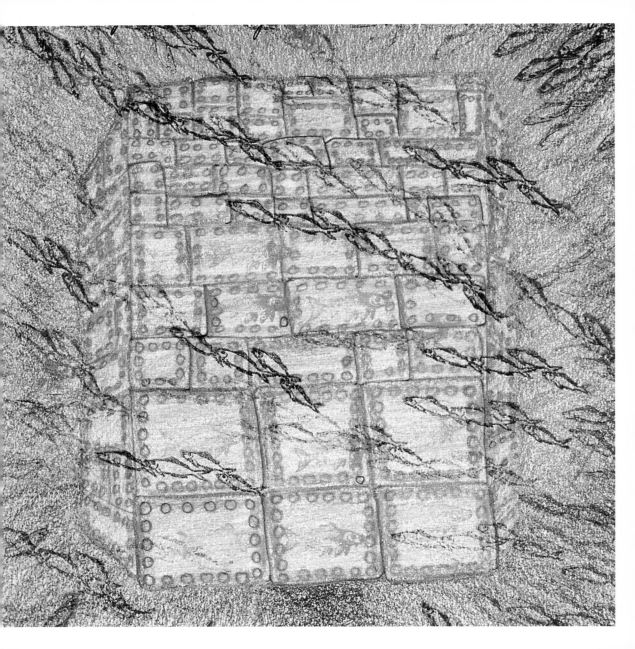

VISION OF ALMA

Losing my mind on paper, I must image this energy.

A silver-haired woman stands in open desert. A poncho of bright spiraling
patterns covers her upper body. Her bare feet rest comfortably in red dirt.
The skin of her face, browned and weathered by sun and wind, is taut and
shiny like steel. Her eyes are brilliant, sapphire blue. In the center of her
forehead is a red dot.

Filled with earth energy, she fills the horizon connecting mesa and sky.
She has borne children and made pots, one of which she holds in her hands.

From the patient geometric patterns of her days come forth words
that spin round her like the spirals on her poncho.

Alma-Mater
Container and weaver,
Woman-spirit within.

I think of O'Keeffe, of Kallowitz, of my grandmother who
loved wild flowers and Navajo blankets and land.

MAGI AND ANIMALS

On the floor of our bedroom, I kneel down on the white shag rug.
Bending my head to the ground in a gesture of prayer, thinking of
Moslems facing east to Mecca, but I am facing south to the laundry room.

Above me shines a circular, silver disc. Delicately carved flowing rhythms
suggest the East, not the West. Figures encircle a symbolic center.
Magi moving toward Bethlehem. In exotic robes, heads enwrapped
in colorful turbans, they approach, reverent and regal.

A tawny lioness lies down beside me. She stirs and starts to prowl, swaying
and showing fiercely gleaming white fangs. I am frightened, but a growl
becomes a cat smile as I stroke her head. She quiets down, flicks her tail,
and moves toward the glass door to the garden. This space is too small.
I open the door to let her out.

As I turn back to the altar, I notice a white tarp covering a large mound.
Slowly I pull it off, exposing dark humus and leaves. From out of this hole
come small blinking creatures. Awakened from sleep, they move toward me,
bewildered—a raccoon, a weasel, a mouse, and a prairie dog.
Each comes from a different place, but one thing they share in common
is hoarding treasure underground.

life on

November 8, 1977

KHN

The tail of this innocent goldfish
fell off to reveal a very old symbol.

FISH BIRTH

Inside a round glass fishbowl, a fancy goldfish with a Baroque tail flutters
frantically above dark stones. Too large for the bowl, she can't breathe
in so little water. My four-year-old son reaches in to pick her up by the tail.
Skin tears loose. The fish drops on the floor. She flops desperately until
I put her back in the bowl. Pain. Fear. Anguish. She will die
of suffocation on the kitchen floor.

A large cut exposes pink flesh along the backbone. Tail separates from body.
In agony she darts around, leaps into the air, and again falls onto the floor.
In death throes, she moans like a frightened little girl.

In the midst of suffering, she turns into my daughter who faces me
wearing white underpants. She places her hand on her sore crotch.
From child to woman *is this the secret?*

ARTSPACE

My artist friend from Larkspur walks in. Joyful welcome. She brings
books on art, women, and myth. One, in particular, stands out.
A thin black composition book with a white square in the middle.
Inside whiteness are swirling reds, greens, yellows, and blues that
flow together in a fluid sphere. In its center is a black oval opening.

My friend and I are close, looking deep into this universe of color.
Her hand presses mine to say something without words, something
larger than friendship, larger than mothering, something about
the warmth of creation.

Surrounding us is my outer world in Utah. Ruggedness, silence,
space above a ring of surrounding mountains. We circle the room
to look at the peaks: the gentle summit of Grandeur Peak
with spring green on its shoulders and dark spruce in its crevices;
the vertical granite thrust of Olympus dusted in snow in its own
cloud-filled air; the distant purple, pink-tipped Oquirrhs across the valley.

Circles shared.

A sharing of art, friendship, and self.

FISHING WITH A HAND-TIED FLY

Below me in a deep circular pool, trout cruise above the stones.
At one end, the pool is dammed.

Three men are fishing. One catches a couple.
The second catches enough for dinner.
The third walks the left bank, carrying a limit
of shining trout on a silver chain.

"How," I ask, "do you do it?"

"The only way," he says, "is with a hand-tied fly."
I think of asking for one, but I know I must learn to make my own.

Now there isn't time, so I catch what I can
on a black-and-white commercial fly.
My cast drops heavily, drifting downstream.
A minnow temporarily hooks itself, but I realize this activity is useless.
I don't want to catch minnows.

RED ROCK SPIRIT

Camping in red-rock country in a soft grassy meadow.
Family and students wander in and out.

In the bottom of a canyon, I look up at giant arches that open
like the Double "O" Arch. Surface ripples and waves from
ancient seas that now stand in air. Suddenly the weather changes.
Strong wind rushes in before a cloudburst. Rain pours from
openings in the rock. Two weeping eyes in a face of stone.

I walk out of the storm into a dark house.
Rooms are littered with printed material and blue books.
A place full of information and conflicting directions.
I begin to poke around, wondering what I'll discover or recover here.

Above me cloud patterns are reshaping
as grayness softens in sun-edged cumulus mounds.

I wonder what the rock sees of the sky.

April 25, 1978

I wonder what's out there in space
as I float in my capsule.

FISHBOWL

In the bottom of a fishbowl punctured with small, square openings like
Le Corbusier's *Chapel at Ronchamp*, I watch colored light pour in
like scattered parts of a rainbow. Floating in space, or heaven maybe,
with no landmarks to guide me in this watery infinity.
I delight in my own levity.

That dreamy, drifting feeling fades as I return to sort shirts
in my husband's closet. On top is a flamboyant crumpled tie.
These men's shirts make me feel uncomfortable.
Machine made, tightly packaged and pinned,
and tossed on a high shelf out of reach.

A   LANDSCAPING   JOB

A friendly, dignified old couple comes to tell me about their house.
The bricks in the lower story are "frozen," crumbling and of poor quality.
They won't support the superstructure. I tell the owner he should
complain to the contractor about the use of cheap foundation materials.
In dread, I wait for the ensuing confrontation.

Soon contractor and crew arrive. They want revenge.
Shovels over their shoulders, they march into our garden to
dig up lilacs, ground cover, young oaks, and maples with
soil clinging to the roots. I let them take the trees because
my comments about "frozen brick" started this war.

After they have tramped off with their plunder, I find
one young oak lying in the road, taproot and branches intact.
Its leaves are bright spring green. I replant it in one of
the holes they have dug, fill it with water and Vitamin B_1
and watch damp soil cover exposed roots.
Renewal after calamity.

A Spanish proverb says, "Every man must have a child,
fight a raging bull, and plant a tree."

So must every woman.

A transplanted tree
needs
Vitamin B-1

"Every man
must have a child,
fight a raging bull,
and plant a tree"
Spanish proverb

Every woman too.

May 22, 1979

The beetles crouch at the bottom in a heap.

December 12, 1979

BUTTERFLY IN A GLOBE

I take out my art history slides to put them into the universal chamber.
My projector bulb is too hot. I begin to remove it from the projector.
Bulb becomes a globe of light. Inside it, insects dart about,
beating their wings to get out—a large black and yellow bee,
a rust-toned butterfly, and dark Mormon beetles at the bottom.

Outside the classroom I shake the globe in air.
The butterfly and the bee are released. The beetles stay in a heap.

NEW LINES FROM AN OLD TREE

High on a steep sage slope, amid low growth on yellow ground,
sits a blonde-haired woman wrapped in a red Tlingit blanket.

"What are you doing?" I ask.

"Putting new lines of communication on the Old Tree."

To my left is an ancient oak with branches that reach out so far
toward the light that some have broken. The woman asks me
how to put a supporting wire in the tree.
I answer by telling Indian legends,
origin and creation myths like the story of Raven.

I wonder why my answer is so far from the question,
but she enjoys my storytelling. Perhaps that is the answer.

New Lives of Communication from an old Tree

The reality of
charred death
rolls down on me.
In facing it I
learn something
wonderful about
living in the energy
of the universe.

July 16, 1980

I am walking a frozen river, stepping over
sheet metal [and] ice plates, [as I]
turn to turn back over my shoulder
the river begins to roar to [underwater]
to [stones] like a [newspaper] frame
falling over [my] [skin] [from] near
death and [experience] of life

KHN

FROZEN RIVER

[An operation to remove a cancer from my right sinus
brings life to a standstill this month.]

Stepping on skid marks, I walk up a frozen river.
White plates of ice crunch underfoot. I turn to see what I've left behind.
The river begins to flow with the murmur of summer.

BLEACHED SKULL

A whitened skull lies on dark earth.
Big eye sockets and reddish horns long buried in red dirt.
Black-white-red. I think of Georgia O'Keeffe's skull in the sky above
the red hills of New Mexico and of white buffalo in the north.

Bones in the desert are swept clear.
That's when they become art.

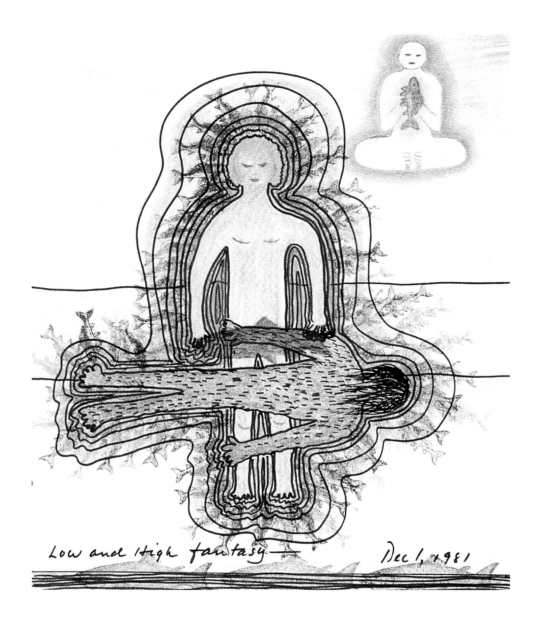

Low and High fantasy —   Dec 1, 1981

HIGH AND LOW FANTASY

In bed next to me, a naked, hairy young man struggles through
drug withdrawal, alternating between restless moaning and sweaty dreams.
Thin, graceful, weak. His grizzled face is shadowed in a two-day growth.
Hair tangled but beautiful, even in this unkempt state. His penis is limp.
Tawny body hair covers his legs and arms like a coyote or rabbit
that has been stretched out or hung.

Waking from a fitful sleep, he gets out of bed and tries to sneak out
while his girlfriend is in the room. "No you don't," I yell at him.
"You'll hurt your friend for nothing. You stay here."

My breath wilts him. His body falls across me,
forming a male/female cross on the white bedsheet.

When the wandering hippie dies, a spirit man appears.
Radiant, silver-haired, silent—my image of wisdom and strength within.
We reach out to each other through touch, not words.
His appearance gives me assurance that all will be well,
at least on the high side of my unconscious.

PLUMBER'S HELPER

The old toilet in the upstairs bathroom is leaking. A new one with
Chinese writing on it is about to be installed.

The head of the humanities department stands opposite me.
White fuzzy hair. A big Santa Claus stomach.
He says confidently, "I can fix it for you."

"I need to call the plumber," I answer. "You have no tools."

Instead of a plumber's helper, he hands me a multicolored bowl
with a superbly decorated domed lid.
Red in the center, encircled by deep blue and
bright yellow with bits of green, its delicate cloisonné enamel
reminds me of Eastern European Easter eggs.
The best of craft and folk art in one form.

It's surprising what unplugs "the head" if you accept the unexpected.

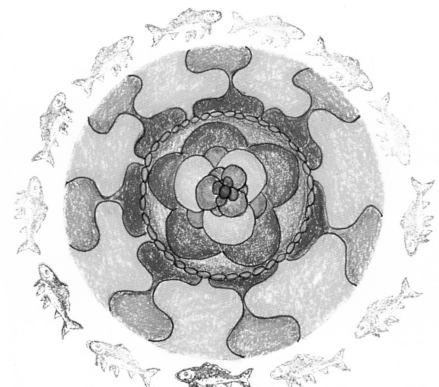

You never know what will unplug you.

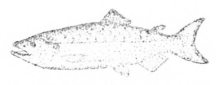

December 8, 1981

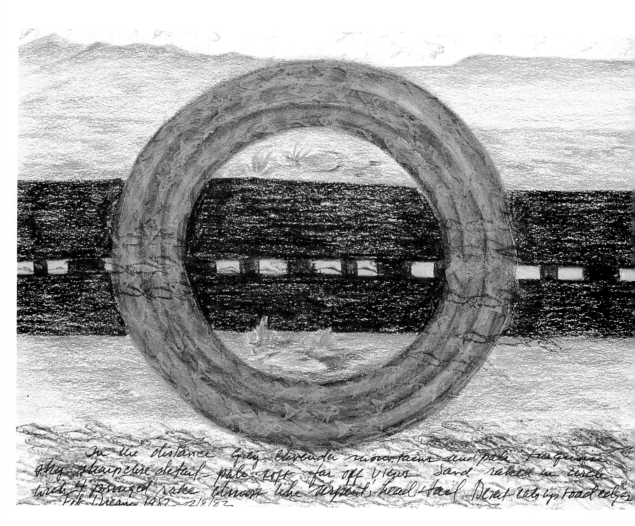

In the distance Grey, lavender mountains and pale turquoise
sky. sharp clear detail pale soft far off views. Sand raked in circle
with 4 pronged rake almost like serpent's head + tail. Desert extends to each edges
Pik. Dreams 1987 2/8/82

ROAD WITHIN A CIRCLE

I walk along a deserted blacktop road in Southern Utah. Scrub, sage,
dry weeds come out of sand. The light is low and clear, casting long shadows
on the ground and making sculpture of the tiniest relief. It is early morning,
early spring. A bare touch of green softens the land.

At my left, stands a weathered wise man in white, loose-fitting clothing.
He knows this country intimately and respectfully.
Together, by the edge of the road, we look at a distant horizon
of pale sky and lavender mountains.

"This can be our home."

"What do you mean?"

I take a bamboo rake to inscribe a circle over the road.

The harmony of my design becomes a shield of self-discovery. The road runs
through the middle with its yellow passing line in the center. Above and below
are semicircles of earth, stones, and green desert plants. The whole is enclosed
within four lines of the rake as it traces a circle of sand over asphalt.

I like this road, seldom traveled, well worn by storm, wind, and blowing sand.
Slowly the desert takes it back, like the circle of sand
that blows across it for awhile.

Reflections come with words; feelings come with colors. Two ways of seeing.

ARTICHOKE PLATE

Alone with a white artichoke plate in my lap,
I stare into the center, a steamed artichoke surrounded by
petal-shaped depressions that are used to catch leftover leaves.
Puns surround me. ART-I-CHOKE!
Peeling off layers of professional life, I try to find the heart inside.

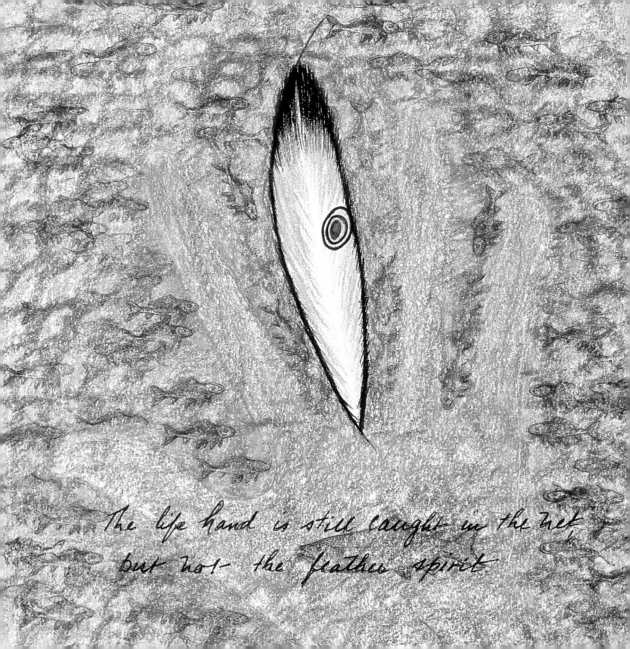

The life hand is still caught in the net,
but not the feather spirit

MAGIC FINGER

On a hill above a small Moroccan town, a horseman in a purple turban
and billowing black pants sits astride a chestnut mare.
He descends into the valley with speed and grace that remind me
of the Arabs in Delacroix's *Lion Hunt*. Galloping between a
sharp-pointed agave and a dark drooping Deodora cedar,
he meets a band of mercenaries below.

They move in to take the village. Horrified, I watch.
Next to me sits a twelve-year-old boy. "If you take away their lifestyle,"
he says, "you must remove their brains. They won't suffer.
It's like unhooking a fish."

Before I can ask why, I am thrust elsewhere.
An artist/writer friend and I are working on a drawing of a right hand.
She draws the outline of a Moroccan good-luck symbol, the sign of Fatima.
Fingers disappear into a blue-violet net that becomes rippling fish scales,
becomes a painted Easter egg. In the end, only the middle finger remains
to form a vagina with a small circular mark where the knuckle was.

"What a slit!" We burst out laughing.

A connection is made by hand between earth and heaven.

NEVADA AND COLORADO

On a Jeep excursion across a dry sheep-grazed sage desert that reminds me
of Nevada, we move fast to catch up with a wedding party, which has
reassembled outdoors for a wedding *sur l'herbe*. As we turn the corner,
I see amazing country on our right. I never realized Colorado
was so beautiful. Majestic snowy crags jut up into azure sky. Below is a deep
pool like the Morning Glory Pool at Yellowstone—clear depths
and cloudy edges. I ask the driver about swimming here.

"You can't," he says. "Scorpions."

We stop the Jeep by the pool. My son approaches between my husband
and a young woman who holds him up. He has cut his right foot.
My husband puts him down at the edge of the pool to bathe his wound.
This water, I realize, is perfectly safe for swimming.

Mountains are sacred at sunrise. The Indians say that one who misses the dawn is dead.

June 10, 1982

AMARETTO

Upstairs in a college library, a dark-haired man tells me that he is glad
I'm coming back to teaching. "You were a great teacher," he says.
"In your class when I asked for a full orchestra, I got one."

I hesitate, pleased with the praise, but my answer is,
"No. I'm not coming back. If it bothers you, write to the president."

A young woman offers everyone a drink from an exquisite, gold-rimmed,
crystal glass filled with Amaretto. In the middle floats a melting ice cube.
I do not drink but pass it on to the man on my left.
I cannot swallow this bittersweet liqueur, at least not in this library.

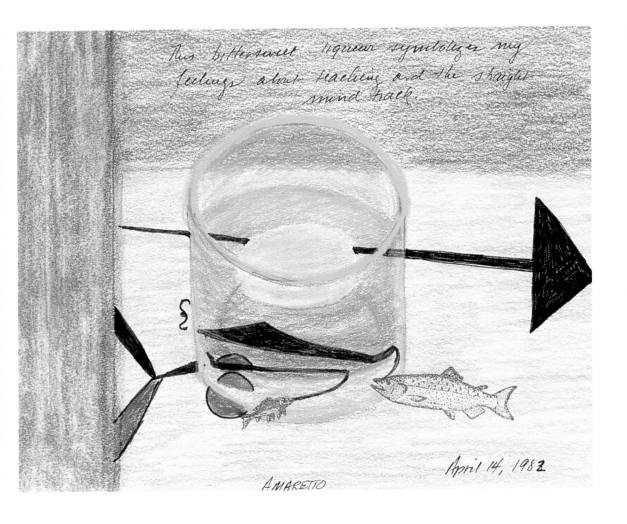

This bittersweet liqueur symbolizes my feelings about teaching and the straight mind track.

AMARETTO

April 14, 1982

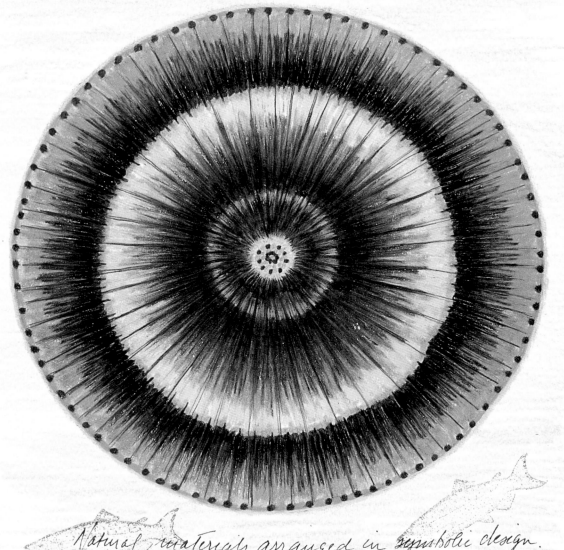

Natural materials arranged in symbolic design.

December 8, 1982

KMN

BRASS RING

The land is gray. It is early winter in the Nevada-Utah desert. A strong wind swirls sand and dust. Our family stops at a weathered ranch house with wooden exterior the same color as the land. I go upstairs to talk with a middle-aged Shoshone woman who is working hides. She has a small box filled with neatly sorted quills, scales, and beads she arranges in symbolic designs on deerskin.
We talk about land and the rituals of her people.
A storm rages. Inside, we barely feel it because the house is so well built.
When the storm lifts, we go on our way.

Later, I'm sitting at a table with my thirteen-year-old son. The Shoshone woman reappears with a younger woman who looks healthy and strong. She sits down opposite me. Why are they here? In answer to my unspoken question, she pulls four pills out of her pocket, one white and three yellow, and hands them to me. "We're not into drugs."
She shrugs and takes them back.

Her daughter comes up to embrace me from behind. I begin to move away half-fighting, half-enjoying the hug. The girl says, "We've got her.
Did you watch her body move?"

Standing at a window ledge again, I face these two women.
The young one reaches out her left hand to take hold of my right arm.
She holds me in a firm grip, a gesture of friendship.

As often, my adventure ends in fishing. I'm in a small boat with my brother-in-law, trying to catch dinner. I have no hook, just a string with a brass ring. Three times I cast into the water. Each time I bring in a fish—a bluegill, a crab, and a fantastically colored perch. I hold the perch above our basket, awed by the intricate pattern of its scales and its dark, shining human eyes.

BATHSHEBA AT BELVEDERE

The managing editor of *Utah Holiday* and I are crossing San Francisco Bay from
Belvedere to Paradise Cove. She wants to swim, but I tell her
we had better go by boat as the currents in Raccoon Straits are tricky.
We arrive at a beach house, dragging a water-soaked air mattress.
All I remember of the house is a painting by Rembrandt,
his darkly glowing *Bathsheba*. Holding a letter from her lover,
her belly full with child, she looks down at her maidservant
and her own bare feet. As body, she is mature, sensual, filled with life.
As soul, she is at another depth far away from the love she
aroused in David, a love for which she will pay dearly.

Rembrandt shows parts of Bathsheba that no one else knows—her feelings
inside about the cost of power and enchantment at a moment of transition.
The choice is hard.

the power of the wave
carries you a long way

July 24, 1983

THE GREAT WAVE

An old friend and I wander through rooms at a party.
We open a door to a courtyard that fills with a rising green wave.
Pointing to its curling crest, I whisper, "Let's ride it together."
My friend comes up behind me as we flow into the curl.
I turn to him, saying, "How good this union feels."
He turns out to be my husband.

T'AI CHI CIRCLE

My T'ai Chi teacher has a gathering at her house in a warm Mediterranean
garden. People of all ages come together in friendly conversation.
The center of attention is an infant. Too young to talk, he claps his hands
and enjoys the party. He reaches for my gloves,
which I am glad to give to him.

Her house is a warm-toned, light-filled mission adobe, surrounded by a verdant
cascading jungle of green plants like Frida Kahlo's garden outside Mexico City.

My teacher and I decide to cycle through her neighborhood on finely tuned
ten-speed bikes. We pedal easily through quiet streets. On our right a double
adobe tower rises up, warm and worn with age. It has seen many lives inside—
country mission, school, and a studio-house. Its most compelling features are
windows that are really paintings, high above the street—a blue sky above a
cloud bank, three gulls circling waves along a shore, and the crosses and domes
of a Baroque Mexican church. Art as windows of the soul reflecting
what is seen from on high, I like that.

My teacher wants to pedal faster, so I pull tight my pedal straps feeling a flow
of strength in my legs as our bikes move forward.
Soon we return, having made a full circle, to rejoin the party.

I have never forgotten the sound of the
bells in Italian Churches, and the dark
cypresses behind the walls of the cloister.
Together they move my insides like
thunder.   January 1, 1983

Sacrifice and Freedom

February

AX IN MY BACK

Laid out on a white sheet on a steel operating table, I see the whole interior,
bare and antiseptic. I lie on my back looking at shadows on the ceiling and a
harsh, blue light overhead. Feeling pressure against my left shoulder, I reach
under me to uncover something cold and hard and sharp. Slowly, carefully,
I remove a red-handled ax. Lowering it to the floor, I see a beautiful view
beyond the window—blue sky above a billowing, wheat-covered hill.
For a moment, or eternity, I float in universe as wheat, as wind.

WEDDING BASKET

My search begins on Belvedere Island, where I played as a child. I ring the bell at the door of a rustic, redwood cabin. A woman invites me in. I tell her that I've come to look for a rug that hung there long ago.

She asks me into the dining room. It's supper time. We sit down to eat at a long refectory table with a couple of children and two middle-aged women. An unusual meal is served—crisp salad in a wooden bowl, special wheat cereal with milk, and an amber-colored drink served in wooden cups. I take the drink to my lips, a marvelous aromatic tea, unlike anything I have ever tasted.

Talk turns to my search. The white-haired woman asks about my family and my past. After listening to my history she says, "That's why you're looking. Your family has collected many things."

As we talk I realize that I'm in the wrong house. I should be on Beach Road, near the water. I thank these women and leave.

In a meadow of dry grass, boxes are scattered on the ground. Woven goods from Mexico, Scandinavia, and the Southwest—things that I am giving away for a civic cause or school benefit. Reaching into one of the boxes, I bring out a Navajo wedding and carrying basket that has traditional marking, but is much deeper. I know this is something special that I must keep until I understand its meaning.

Meanwhile dogs wander through the grass. One pair is tied to a leash held by a blind man—a dark yappy dog and a big Seeing Eye dog. Someone cuts them loose to quiet them. The blind man is glad. As I look at his clear, penetrating eyes, I wonder if he only pretends blindness.

The spinning of the universe

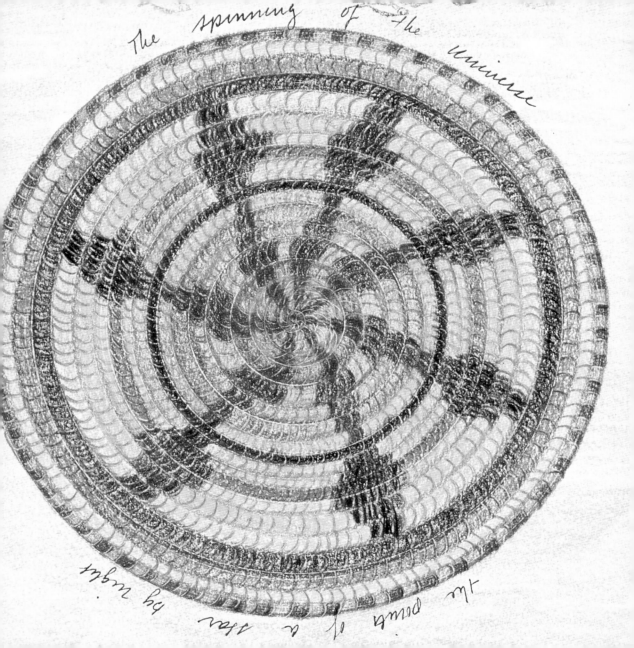

the growth of a star by night

Explosion becomes flower. the spirit
floats again in peaceful
waters.

EXPLOSION

Wounding goes on until I am both wounder and wounded.

I am about to give a lecture at 2:00 on modern art. The woman at the
scheduling desk says only a few people have signed up, but the business
management lecture before mine is filled with docile males taking notes.
My lecture never takes place as I move through a life-gripping experience
I must repeat to get the point.

Down a crowded narrow street in New Delhi, a dark Moslem wearing a black
turban walks on my right. We hesitate in front of Gandhi's house and throw a
bomb. After the explosion, I wander in a daze, stunned by what I've done.

Again we walk by the house. Again the Moslem throws an explosive.
The building splinters and bursts into flames. We separate. I am devastated.
I return to the site of the explosion and turn myself over to the police.
My accomplice is at the police station, too. He announces, without remorse,
"I'm leaving the country." Guilt and sadness overwhelm me,
but he walks off with ease. What brass balls!

The only way to heal the explosion is to draw. Ashes and splinters of black
become a flower of purple with a white soul-center. Anger becomes art.

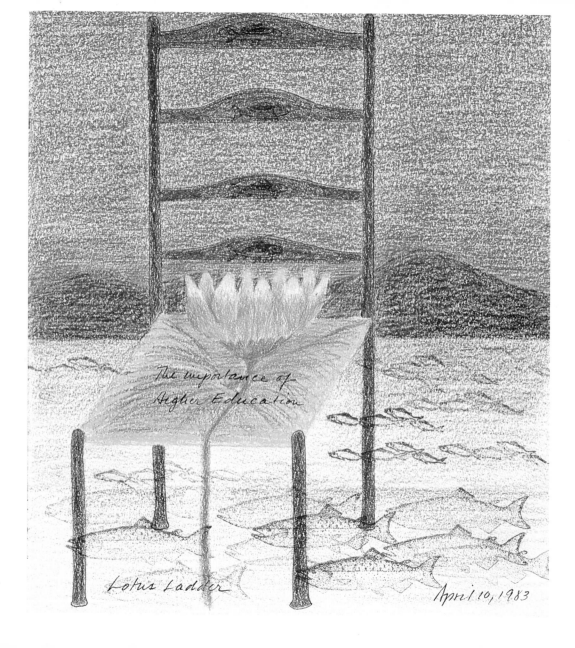

The importance of
Higher Education

Lotus Ladder

April 10, 1983

FLYING FISH AND LOTUS I

Large stone steps lead to the entrance of a house made of hand-hewn logs.
A rough rock wall surrounds this simple, well-constructed fortress.
Behind the house are corrals for horses, a fruit orchard, and a
large vegetable garden. Traces of days lived close to seasons and
animals with a natural reverence for life.

Beyond the corral, I walk to a low bank overlooking a deep pool. Three times
I cast in a muddler minnow. I know a fish is there. Finally, I hook one very
gently on the lower lip. I pull it in, rest it on the ledge awhile, and return it
to the water. It is a very unusual fish, a hybrid carp and trout with bronze scales
on its body and delicate transparent fins that flutter like rainbow wings.
On its head, moving lumps make it seem to wrinkle its wise brow.
Its eyes are soft, deep brown.

With my children and my sister's children, I return to my grandmother's house
for the night. The boys sleep downstairs, the girls on the second floor.
I go up to the third floor. The housekeeper says to me, "If you want to
practice yoga, this is a special quiet room, above it all."
I don't practice yoga, but I like the inner space.

11

Before retiring, I talk with my grandmother who looks younger than
I remember her. Since she is flying to India in the morning, she says,
"You can use the whole house." How extensively she has redone the interior.
It is fresh and colorful—new paint, floral paper, hand-painted beds and bureaus
in a moving sea of yellow, pale green, lavender, and blue.
Inside, this place feels like springtime in Frida Kahlo's bright, yellow kitchen.

Outside, I stand on a lakeshore in evening light with an artist/librarian friend.
We talk about the importance of higher education, not university degrees
but degrees of higher learning in life. She holds out a pink lotus, which she
places on the straw seat of a French provincial ladder-back chair.

Beyond the ladder, we watch a dark, bearded man who stands knee deep
in the lake. Balancing his energies, he stamps his feet and beats his chest,
splashing water over his naked body in a self-baptism ritual.
His face reminds me of a policeman-student I once taught,
who in midlife switched from law enforcement to humanities.

Now he has something to teach me.

Across the lake, evening backlights the mountains with turquoise and rose. The
lotus glows salmon pink in the darkness. Like the evening, it is edged in gold.

A sacred, shimmering spirit from
the deep.

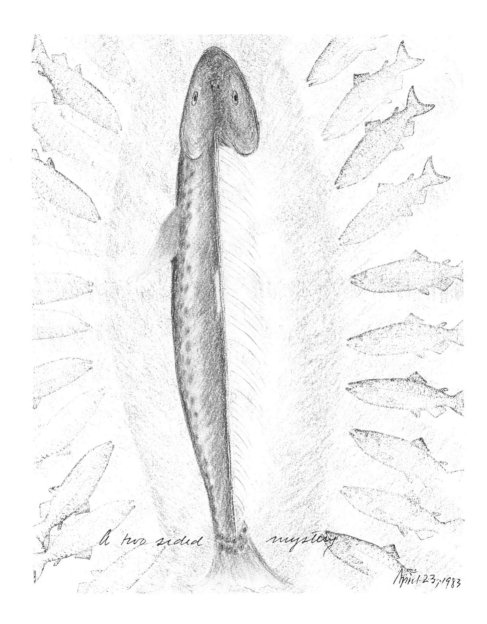

A two sided mystery

April 23, 1983

HALF A FISH

Now even the fish is wounded.

Standing by a mountain stream, I look deeply into a pool in which a
huge steelhead floats. Cramped in a space that is too small, it is still as death.
Holding it by its tail in air, I see its right half eaten to the bone.
All that remains is a white skeleton with meager fragments of pink flesh.
I am frozen in shock and numb despair.

Even with only half its body left, this fish is tremendous and heavy with meat,
more than enough for my husband and me to eat. I'm afraid the flesh
may be spoiled, but he says it died in cold, clear water, so the meat,
chilled in the river, will be fresh.

He fillets the left side, and we share an underwater gift.

INSIDE MY MOLAR

Beyond green-and-white wrought-iron gates is a carriage lane lined with
giant chestnut trees. I think of Voltaire's estate where he watched
high-class ladies catch their precariously high, powdered wigs in
the branches of his chestnuts as they walked toward him.

I park and walk down the lane into an inn with an interior paneled in
dark wood. With me I carry a leather suitcase filled with black clothing
I take to the basement to have washed. The laundress tells me not to put
clothes that are delicate in the washing machine.
I take out a black silk cocktail dress and a plastic raincoat.
Everything else goes in.

Returning to my room, I begin to pull at my molar, which becomes
a marvelous pink-and-white cavity: iridescent, opalescent, womb-like.
Inside is a fabulous sculpture garden that shimmers like a
soap bubble and a seashell. Through pinks, deep magenta, and pearly white,
I wander in delight, feeling curves and hollows and watching light
slide over smooth surfaces into velvet shadows.

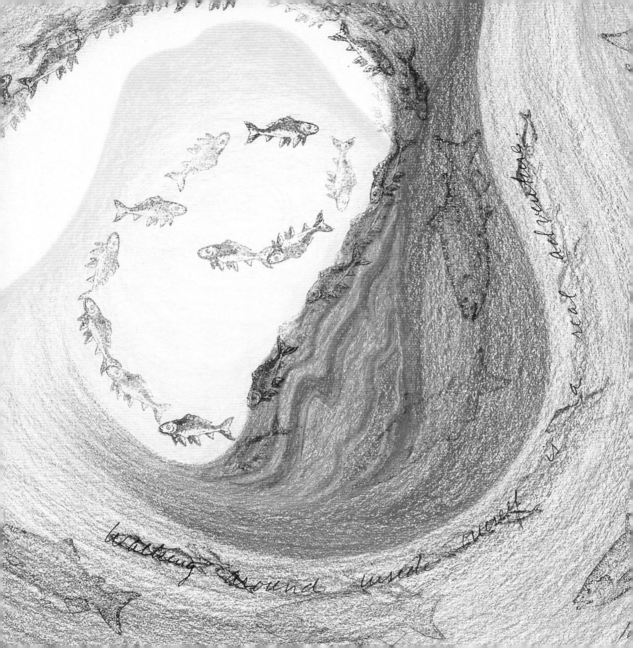

A l'alta fantasia qui
mancò possa,
Ma già volgeva il mio
disiro e'l velle
Sì come rota ch'
igualmente è
mossa,

L'amor che move
il sole e l'altre
stelle.
— Paradiso —

May 26 1987

Book of poems
opened at
the middle.
Radiant yellow
tulip in a glass womb.
A frying pan from which
I scrape spaghetti sauce.
I think how beautiful
the flower is, how
I must clean the pan
after feeding the family.
But really I must
recite these long
passages from an
ancient epic,
and ...

KHN

ANCIENT BOOK OF DAYS

A book is opened in the middle of a long poem, a divine comedy of daily life.
Beside it, in the background, a green glass vase holds a yellow and orange
Rembrandt tulip. Farther away is a frying pan out of which I scrape
spaghetti sauce for the children before turning the pan into a full moon.

I begin to recite from this book in an ancient language I didn't know I knew.
Long passages from many cultures that I have brought together.
Between words I see the breathing of the tulip and the moon,
and I remember that I must clean up after feeding the family.

Underneath it all,
the recitation
of a long-
forgotten
language
moves me
profoundly.

ESSENCE

In the midst of lecture projects, conversations, and children's arrangements,
I sit face-to-face with a middle-aged woman who tells me her dream journey.
I am surrounded by symbols. At the center is a gray figure enwrapped
like a mummy. Through bandages, eyes stare from inside out.
Placing this form on the table between us, she says, "This is the essence."

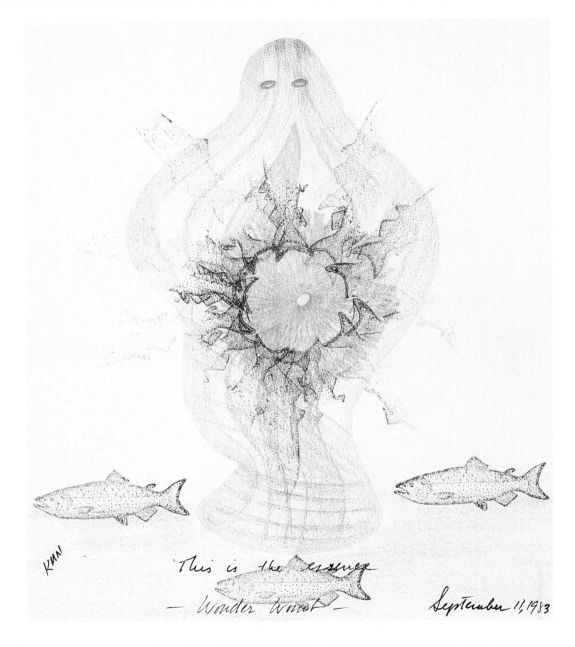

KMN

"This is the essence

— Wonder Worst —

September 11, 1983

September 18, 1983

Many layered yet exposed

steel and radiant warmth

SOPHIA

Once again I am in the middle of a party routine amid nervous talk.
People move from room to room, drifting on the edge of
fragmented conversations. In the center sits a woman, still as stone.
I think of Sophia Loren, but this woman's powers
go way beyond physical beauty.

She sits half-naked behind a red translucent triangle and fine veil of gauze.
Multi-layered but not covered up, she is self-contained in contrast
to the surrounding chitchat and changing personae that drift past her.
Radiance within. Cool steel on the surface.
Her blue eyes see through everything.

The essence unwrapped. What a birthday gift.

POOL OF TRUTH

It is late at night. Police lights flash in darkness around a massive accident
at an intersection. Naked bodies are strewn across the road.
I think of Gericault's *Raft of the Medusa*, a wreck at sea that reduced
political idealism to cannibalism. Destruction and pain. Nausea floods me
as I turn in the opposite direction, sickened by this devastating confusion
of gas, blood, steel, and flesh.

Descending spiral stairs to a ground-level patio, I meet mothers and daughters
who talk about charity and friendship. I wish I could believe this
Mormon sermon of "good-sister" values, but I feel uneasy in this space.

We are handed round cakes and told, "Throw a piece into the pool of truth
and ask a question." My three friends ask questions about life and love,
but I cannot. I throw my cake into the pool and suddenly out pops,
"Should I paint?"

No answer.

Below me, stairs covered with skins of white bears lead to a lower level.
As I go down, I feel a sharp biting pain in my left hand. Taking my hand
off the rail, I step carefully over the sleeping polar bears.

William Blake

the image of truth

anything capable of being imagined

Pool of Truth

Trees are   better teachers
than books   or people. They
don't ask   questions you
can't answer. They are
    for self-reflection, reaching
down into earth and up
        into air.

R E T U R N   T O   T H E   T R E E

Fall leaves bring up a recurring dream of an aspen tree in a saddle
between two hills. It is October. Earth darkens beneath flecks of gold.
A thousand black-eyed Susans stare up into the sky. Their browning leaves
rattle as I walk through them toward a white aspen in the middle
of a clearing. Its branches are thin lines against the blue,
a gold crown of leaves lies at its base. Slender, stripped bare,
its skin is cool and smooth to touch. I stand naked, like the tree,
and take hold, flowing into intercourse with earth and trunk and sky.
I love and am in love with this tree. The whole of life surges up
from my bare feet, putting me in touch with all that's above and below.

I now know why lovers leave their mark on the aspen's bark.

TREE - WOMAN

I walk upstairs to a studio-loft, carrying a six-foot piece of lumber. In the center
is a stained glass figure of a red-haired Renaissance woman dressed in flowing
robes. She reminds me of a birthday gift—the personification of the month of
Settembre, a Florentine woman in the center of a dish. In her arms she holds a
basket filled with the full harvest of late summer and early fall.
The ripeness of earth gathered in maturity.

Balancing this cumbersome two-by-four, I make my way upstairs and
gently lay the tree-woman on the floor of the studio where she belongs.

Outside the studio, I crawl through a dark cypress. Branches spread out low to
the ground. I remember trees I used to climb in the Presidio of San Francisco.
Secret places for creative imagination and making pots in a house
of dark boughs. Beyond the tree-house is a magnificent view
of the Golden Gate above late afternoon fog.

A child in a tree house and a Renaissance woman encased in lumber
share common roots. Art is what connects them.

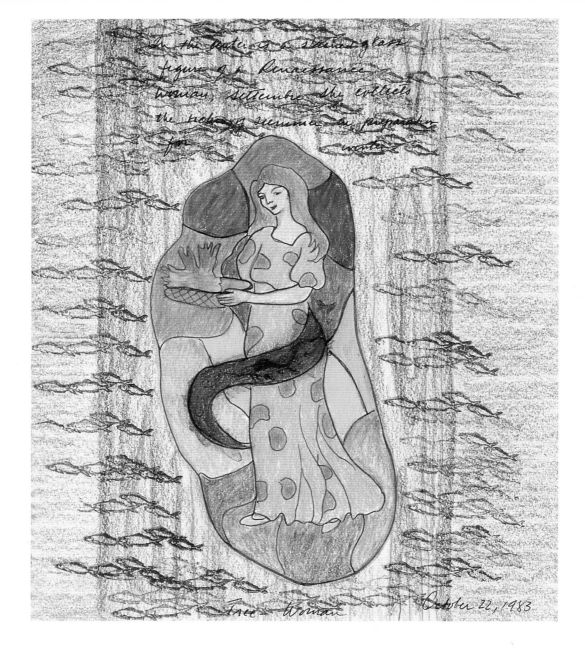

In the water is a stained glass
figure of a Renaissance
woman, sitting she collects
the rich of summer in preparation
for winter

Free Woman   October 22, 1983

Descent to the Goddess appears with a new cover — a blue dolphin from the Queen's megaron in the ancient Cretan palace at Knossos. She rises with elegant power.

October 29, 1983

ASCENT OF THE DOLPHIN

In the process of changing clothes in a dimly lit tunnel, I hear the phone ring.
On the other end is a childhood friend from California.
She faces big changes in her life, but like me, she waits in conflict.
She needs *Descent to the Goddess.* I begin to answer, "I'm too busy to get it," but I
hear deep emotion in her voice. Her words break in tears,
and I know I have to get the book for her.

Out of nowhere, it appears with a new cover. In the center of a dark field,
a brilliant blue dolphin rises on its tail. One of those glorious,
curving creatures on the walls of Knossos who comes from
the heart of sacred power in the queen's megaron. Up through the ages
she swims from Cretan to Christian mythology, the strongest,
swiftest of water creatures who carries the soul to the world beyond water.

CLINGING CRAB

In an aquamarine full-length evening gown, I prepare to give a lecture,
but feel too done up in formal society attire for this job.
At my feet is an upside-down crab that pulls at the hem of my dress.
I hear its claws tear at the satin as it moves backwards. I have to stop
and pay attention to its pull. I remove the crab from my hem
and set it right side up. It scuttles off in a sideways dance.

Why is a crab at my feet while I lecture? Frightened and fascinated,
I know the strength of its claws, its determination to hang on.

She scuttles across the sand...

... words across the night sky, on Cancer

Crab on the edge   Carole 30, 1983

Stellae Maris   November 13, 1983

STAR CANOE

Alone on the edge of a beach in gray light at the edge of night and day,
a shiny ebony canoe waits with small stars scattered on her sides.
Ready for an extraordinary journey, she brings forth the image of Nut,
Egyptian goddess of the night sky stretched over earth. Her bow
pushes forward into darkness with a single black paddle in her belly.
Inside her, one can travel to the edge of the world.

TATTOO OF
TRANSFORMATION

Light slants through the bedroom shutters, weaving a pattern of
regularly alternating light and dark, as I sit at my writing desk, weaving
word patterns for a lecture. I look down at my left arm in amazement.
The underside is an elaborate tattoo-web of fine black lines.
A labyrinth with a central opening near the top from which emerges
a small green disc. I think of spider webs holding beads of water
at intersections, of star maps marking constellations, of a carapace,
of a scarab, of a street plan for an ancient city surrounding a central forum.

Making connections of imagination, map becomes constellation,
becomes pot, becomes scarab with one bent wing.

A labyrinth became a star map, a map a tattoo, and finally a scarab locking a pit transforming its to a star map.

FEAR AIR/PORT

A bag of colors,
of Questions,
of infinite possibility

November 25, 1983

MEDICINE BAG

On the way out of an Anasazi exhibit, I see a mysterious buckskin pouch
shaped like a keyhole. Stitched around the edges with rawhide thongs,
its center is a landscape of mesa country with a cow standing in sage.
At the bottom is a cryptic message: "Fear Air/Port."

I wake up holding this pouch, and remembering what
Agnes Whistling Elk said, "When you make your bag, keep it simple."

That's good medicine!

THREE WOMEN IN ONE

Standing in the lobby of the St. Francis Hotel in San Francisco,
I visit with two high-powered friends who are done up in polish,
jewels, and stylish clothes.

Overwhelmed by their sophistication,
I shrink to a little Alice in Motherland,
lying curled up on the left breast of a nursing mother.
She is smooth and firm and soft. The turn of her head shows
the strength of her neck and the graceful curve of her shoulder
as she stretches out her arms east and west.
Drifting into her warmth, I am once a worshiper in an ancient earth shrine,
and a small, loving child who is still connected to her mother's breast.

Of the three, it's woman stretched out on earth as earth that holds me.

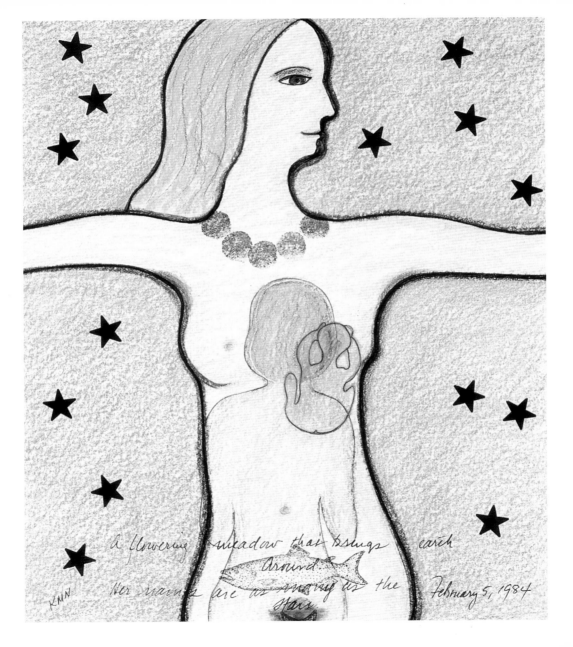

A flowering meadow that brings earth
around
Her names are as many as the stars.

KMN   February 5, 1984

soft Moroccan underneath.

strongly patterned Navajo
above

DIAMOND PATTERN

At a birthday celebration, women friends from school share lunch
in a flowering garden. Iceland poppies, daffodils, and lilacs are shaded
by a majestic persimmon tree and ancient California oak.

As I walk through the garden, a friend from childhood rushes up to hug me.
"You're wonderful," she says. How good it feels to be acknowledged
just for being one's self.

We walk into the living room where there is something I want to show her.
I throw down a Navajo rug over a softly colored Moroccan one.
A strongly patterned black border surrounds a white field.
Lightning zigzags enter from the four corners, flashing toward a red diamond.
Black, white, red: it fills my field of vision and my thoughts.

Red diamond becomes passionate embrace as my husband's face meets mine
through years of caring, sharing, struggle, and surrender.
Friendship beyond words.

SELF-PORTRAIT DONE BY HAND

This is a clear message, needing little explanation.
A wounded right hand rises out of water into air—the opening
of self—sore insight.

"The healing is in the wound."

Mountain of love opened wide becomes an eye.

Mountains of fire opened and became
an eye,
Between earth and sky.

February 1984

The healing is in the wounding

The northern part of the walls
seemed sleeping, but undisturbed.
This part of fascinating, an
archaeological adventure, that
leads toward the tunnels of
the ancient city of stones
was filled.   February 22

ROMAN SUBSTRUCTURE

An old friend and I walk together through a rough, watery landscape
of ochres and midnight blue. We travel a circle, talking about children,
lovers, husbands, women's energy, and intuition. Along the way,
she weeps over human and creative moments lost.

We return to our beginnings to descend through an arched gateway
into the ruins of a Roman basilica that has endured, though often torn apart.
After looking around above, I go down through the arch into the bowels
of an older, vaster civilization. A place of stone, not video.
The first part of my journey seemed tentative and distracted
but the second part, the descent, is compelling.

URSA MAJOR

Wandering around upstairs, I glimpse a dark shape on the porch, hear heavy
feet on the deck, and I turn toward the front door. What used to be a
Sheetrock wall is now a large bay window. From the other side, a brown bear
stares at me. She looks tired, like a mother emerging from hibernation.
An animal from the-looks-within-place, she is fierce in her protection of her
cubs and her nights of heavy sleep. Through her I am connected to the dark
and to the stars. Upstairs I pass a white bathroom. In the middle of whiteness,
an oblong stone, like an Apache tear, sits inside a brown striped seashell—a
luminous talisman of earth and water suspended in midair.

Beyond the bathroom, I meet an unknown woman in a de Chirico train station.
It is late afternoon—yellow light, yellow arches, sharp angles of shade.
She walks toward me across the shadowed piazza. Her soft blonde hair
matches her beige wool suit. Around her neck she wears a dark brown ribbon
over a white silk collar. We embrace. I feel a rush of warmth as I rest my head
against her. How fine she is, how understated in her intensity. When I tell her
how I feel, she hugs me, saying only one word, "Quality."
How much experience, discipline, and personal courage goes into quality
if one wears it with ease.

I am surprised to see that we are wearing the same suit. When I mention this,
she laughs. "Of course," she says, and we walk off to get her luggage.

The Bear comes from the "looks within" place. Sometimes
hibernation is the only way to get ready for spring.

March 9, 1984

My Grandmother's Ring

When the ring fits everything fits together.

My Ring   April 6, 1984

MY GRANDMOTHER'S RING

My husband and I are looking through cases in a small jewelry store. I notice a pale green ring with the lion of St. Mark on it. I slip it on my little finger to admire the light coming through the stone. My husband wants to buy it for me, but it's a school ring, which I don't want.

Why am I looking at jewelry? That's not my style.

Still I stand at the counter opposite the jeweler. Something is in the back of my mind. Suddenly I remember. From my pocket I pull out an antique piece of gold inlaid with diamonds—a cylinder ring with a cluster of precious stones forming a diamond design in the center. The ring has been cut down the back and flattened into a family crest. I want to have this ring enlarged and repaired to fit my finger. The jeweler measures my ring finger and says he needs to add gold. It will be ready in the afternoon.

I am excited to wear a ring that was my grandmother's. She had to have it cut off her hand when, as an old woman, her fingers were swollen with arthritis.

Meanwhile, my husband and I start off along a rocky coastline, enjoying the climb between beach and cliff. Along the way we meet a red-haired woman who invites us to her house on the point. Inside, her house is a Fauve painting come to life: wild walls, upholstery, and even bedsheets. Patterns of yellow, pink, avocado, persimmon, Aegean blue. It's almost overwhelming but fantastic fun. I decide to bed down here, crawling in between sheets of yellow, red, pink, and green. What dreams I could have in this bed. Night would be brighter than day.

FOUNTAIN

In both hands I hold a multicolored kinetic fountain,
encased in a bell jar. Around this fountain cluster events and interactions.
My daughter and I go to Snowbird for a late spring ski in the upper valley.
Below I meet a lift operator who is working on the lower lift, which is
temporarily broken. A handsome middle-aged man dressed in sturdy
workman's clothes says in a friendly voice, "I'll take you where you have to go."

We start off across a snow field. "Watch out!" I scream as he passes the road
scraper on the right. "It's okay," he says as we drive through a sharp-angled,
sharp-edged metal gateway to a cafe.

Sitting at the counter next to him, I lean back, reaching for the sugar and
ending up in his embrace. As my behind pushes against his crotch, he says,
"What a fine ass you have." This encounter is exciting but only half explored.
Leaving the cafe d'amour, I look up into high strands of spring clouds.
Feeling a warm wind on my body, I remember his touch and what the
Mexican women say about the "wind of the unconscious."

Later, I am back in the kitchen, fixing food for the family. My red-haired
mother gossips with my aunt at the table. Grandchildren wander in and out.
I lean forward toward the two of them saying, "I want in on the gossip."
Laughing, we lower our voices, which immediately brings in a curious child.
My aunt whispers in my ear, "Your daughter is the one. She has it all."

I remember the dream of her handing me the magic pencils, her courage when
stranded in a foreign land, her wounded right hand. She has given me more
than I will ever be able to acknowledge.

The spirit of the fountain never dies

April 26, 1984

Katherine Nelson

MY EGYPT

I am in an auditorium listening to President Reagan spout his usual party line,
punctuated with smiles. Afterwards, there are more questions from the floor.
We exchange ideas. He asks for my name, which I write on a scrap of paper
and hand over to him. I'm surprised at my acquiescence, but not his
"old movie star" version of friendliness that comes across without any real feeling.

What is this scrap of paper with my married name on it? An official name for
an official. As I begin to sign my name, I am angry at seeing myself
as a scrap for a president. To counteract the signature of my persona,
I copy my sacred name as it appears on an ankh sign.
Katherine begins with Ka (life spirit) and ends with the water glyph.
Between is the feather of Ma'at, the sign of right order. My Egypt.

RAINBOW POT

After running around in semi-darkness, doing errands, I am alone.
A voice says, "Write with feeling."

A hand-built stoneware pot that I made in Mississippi fills the space.
Inside are my magic pencils.

Write with feeling?
Right with feeling?
Rite with feeling?

write with feeling

May 3, 1984

It would be wonderful to read a bible of an individual journey rather than the propaganda of a culture ladened with lessons and dogma.

OLD TESTAMENT OR NEW?

In the midst of many pickups, deliveries, and dream confusions, I see a man at
the writing desk. In front of him is a thick book. He works steadily writing in
his tome, like one of the evangelists preparing an illuminated manuscript:
the scribe who passes on sacred symbols and scripture.
But this man is not from the Middle Ages. He is from our time.
Dressed in a conventional Madison Avenue gray-flannel suit,
he sits at his desk, writing on and on. In his right hand he holds
an aqua-colored pencil. On his third finger, he wears a silver ring.

This book is his life as well as others who lived in earlier times.
It will continue after his chapters end.

GRAND HOTEL

We have been traveling *en famille* for a long time. Everyone is tired and
short-tempered, suffering from station-wagon rear end, a disease of
suburban summers. We find a hotel in Paris. My daughter asks me,
"Oh, please, Mom, can we stay?"

"I'll have to ask your grandmother." I phone her room. It's okay. We stay.
I'm glad we're not moving for a while. I want time to look around.
Below me is a well-kept garden with flowers planted in geometric patterns
like the Tuileries. Through the doors of our balcony, white curtains flutter
in shuttered sunlight over shadows and reflections of the Second Empire.
I think of the last days of the carriage trade before honking cars and
blinking streetlights, of Paris along the jetty, as Seurat painted her in a
gentle neo-impressionistic dream.

This room is familiar. Have I lived here before, in another life, perhaps,
or merely in a dream?

Gentle breezes blow through white
curtains bringing the smell of summer
into the room.

The Old Hotel

June 5 1984

PUBLIC EVENTS VERSUS SNAKES FROM INDIA

I walk through a gray, domed public events center, looking for a bathroom
in which to urinate and wash my hands. On the way out of the ladies' room,
I meet a Mormon art-educator-administrator to whom I have brought
information on Utah art. She is friendly, but we are miles apart,
going in different directions.

Later I am at home in my study when the phone rings. "It's from India."
Who do I know in India? I rush to the phone. It's my German friend who is
translating letters of Jung for an analyst. She is ecstatic, describing an erotic
body-snake bas-relief that she has seen. Dark snakes weave in and out of each
other; female bodies stretch upward toward a red disc.
I think of pre-Raphaelite paintings, of Jean Deville's *Treasures of Satan*.
The flow of life writhing around women's bodies as they curve and thrust
upward. In their midst is a young male caught up in this surge of feeling.

ON THE MOVE

I feel a relentless determination to move on and a deep sense of loss.
I stand alone, surrounded by the whole Indian nation, who circles the horizon.
They are gathered together to travel on once again. This time, where
will they go? They have been pushed to the edge of the continent,
to the edge of the circle. As I listen to their talk, guilt floods me—the
underside of manifest destiny and missionizing Catholicism. Broken treaties,
blankets, booze, burned orchards—the "Lords of the Earth"
versus Spanish and American governments.

It's time to move.

I return to an old frontier hotel in Colorado to begin my own ritual of renewal.
In both hands I hold a green plant in a green plastic container. I bend down
over the toilet to place my plant just above the water in the bowl. Holding it in
my left hand, I sprinkle its leaves with my right. Four times I scoop up water
and listen to it drip back through earth to water.

At first I don't want to touch the toilet water, but my feelings change
as I look down into the clear, white basin. I know it's pure.

I burst out laughing as my high view of self comes to earth.
I always thought revelation would come by the infinite sea or on a peak
beneath endless sky, not in the toilet bowl. *C'est la vie.*

"The fifth Way of learning is through Mother Earth herself"
Seven Arrows

Close your eyes

Neale Tree

The perfect Tree

Keep your picture

inside.

July 24, 1984

PERFECT TREE

I stand at the edge of the ocean, watching three figures move through
waves toward the beach. Two wear snorkels. One carries a leopard shark
whose gill openings he squeezes as he emerges from the surf. He raises it
in the air and returns it to the sea. At first I am afraid, but watching him
tells me that his aggressive behavior is mere bravado.

Seashore changes to golf course where I am about to play in a society
tournament. After much activity, I find the hole where I am to begin.
It is not on the fairway where you'd expect, but in a room
with a black chest that sits on a Persian rug.
I ask a young woman, "Where does this hole go?" She is angry that
I don't know. Since there is a long wait, I decide to find out for myself.
This requires a long walk, a boat ride across a lake in California, and,
finally, my return to take my turn in the tournament.

Reaching into my bag for my leather golf glove, I pull out a black, oblong
container with perforated edges. Inside are paper designs with handprints and
landscapes on them. I have mixed emotions. I can't play golf with this
equipment, but I'm excited at the discovery of these mysterious images.
Inside a black border is a natural scene divided internally into five levels.
In the center is a delicate outline of an open hand.
Tarot, Moroccan good-luck sign, hands in prayer?
My fascination with symbols makes me forget the game. As I draw them,
I realize how oriental they are. An asymmetrical tree branch
reaches up from water below to sky above through the five levels.

As the Zen master said, "Close your eyes. Wipe clean your mind.
Now think tree. The perfect tree. Keep your picture inside
and prune your Bonsai to fit your picture."

POLARIS COMPASS

Beside a stream, everything is quiet. A sleek German brown circles in a pool
beneath me. She wiggles across a gravel bar toward my feet.
Noises downstream startle her. Gliding away, she turns into a spotted seal.
To her left is a beaver that slaps its tail and disappears, too.

Finally I'm at a dinner ceremony in a Masonic lodge with my fisherman friend
who recently joined the order. I am surprised that he buys into all the vows and
rituals of this group—politics and institutional religion mixed in deadly earnest.

After we eat, he gives me "the sacred text" and a Polaris compass. A silver
pointer whose center is a wheel that is used for orientation above and below.
Turning it in both hands, I wonder what it all means.

I think of Blake's "Ancient of Days," bending over the globe with his cosmic
compass; of the polestar, Alpha Ursa Minor, the guiding star for earth; of the
Polaris pin given out at Four Winds Camp to those who know how to set their
course at sea and use the winds.

A compass is used to find one's way in new territory. I like that.

I turn the compass in both hands,
pointing to the sky above and to
the earth below.

September 4, 1984

— Pole Star Compass —

Finally I go way down to the bottom of my underwater realms. My husband and I are watching speckled trout swim in gravel pits. He says we should go down to see the fish. Our descent begins. First through the ponds, then to an underwater chamber. Now I am alone. As I turn the corner I come face to face with a hairy beast who walks toward me. He is huge, very strong. He starts to take my arm. I pull away, moving through a passage way to the right. I feel like Alice in Waterland, and am frightened, feeling beyond my depth. I am not ready to kiss the beast into a shining prince. At least I found out where he lives inside me.

It's time to return to the land above the pond, and to start another chapter in my <u>Night Journey</u>.

KHN

BOTTOM OF THE POND

My husband and I watch speckled trout cruise the shallows of a gravel pit.
"We should go down to the level of the fish," he says.

Our descent begins. But I go lower, alone, to an underwater chamber where
I come face-to-face with a hairy bear that grabs at my arm. In fright,
I turn away, trying to walk-swim up through a narrow passage.

Before me, beast becomes teddy bear as I draw its watery form.
Through waves of colored pencils on white paper floats a memory that
takes me back to childhood, to the basement where my mother stored
my stuffed animals because "I was being selfish."
For years they were left downstairs.

At the bottom, in the basement of the dream,
are the abandoned instincts of childhood.

A VIEW INSIDE

I see inside an opening into a white circle. At the center is a small black dot
from which eight black lines radiate like spokes of a wheel or marks
on a compass. This circle floats in night clouds lit by a moon.
Mysteriously veiled on the edges, it is divided evenly between earth and air.

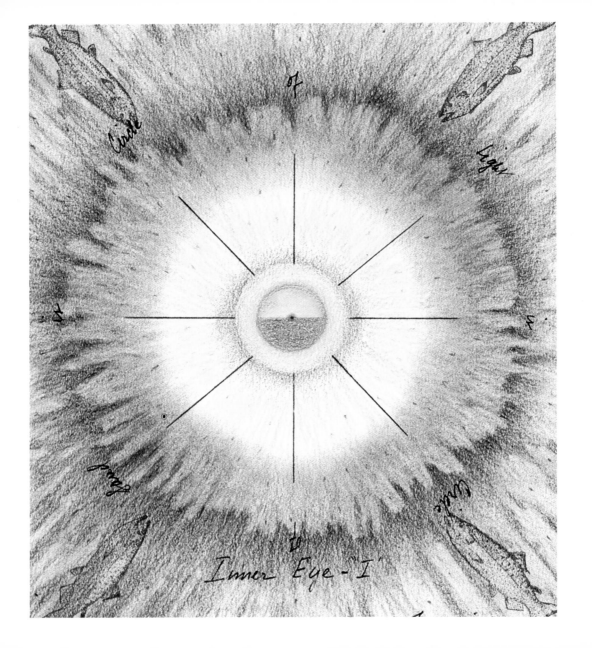

Inner Eye - "I"

ESPRESSO

I am in a small grocery store, picking carefully through the tomatoes, onions,
garlic, and peppers. The vegetables are natural, not supermarket perfect:
sun-ripened, with a few scars from branches and bugs. My selection is pears.
The grocer, a burly, robust man, asks, "What can I show you?" I can tell by his
hands and his tone of voice that he is Italian, so I answer in Florentine dialect.
He is delighted to converse *per un momentino* in his native tongue.

Since I have lived in Italy, he insists that I come with him to his country church.
"La chiesa é Methodiste," he says, *"ma come in Italia, non come in America."*

He takes off his grocer's apron, and we take off up a winding mountain road to
a small building with a tile roof. Across the entrance, *Espresso* is written in bright
pink. Inside, the decoration is Sicilian. Dark hand-carved furniture, richly
colored tapestries, and a few heavy brass candleholders emboss the interior.
The grocer-priest goes off to change into his robes. An old, thin Italian
leads me upstairs to the auditorium where the celebration takes place.

I anticipate a drab service with intermittent singing and preaching to grind
down the soul. That's certainly not what Espresso is all about. Young members
of the congregation scatter across the floor, dressed in their Sunday best,
as the beat begins from loudspeakers at the back of the room.

The rhythm of the music changes with the rhythm of the dancers, who chant,
"Sia Fuoco. Sia Vente. Sia Terra. Sia Aqua. Sia Verme. Sia Uccello.
Sia Bestia. Sia." This is a real holiday as people leap, wriggle, swim,
and float through space. Body and soul are one in fun.
Playing in ceremony is not standing on it. *Magnifico! Viva l'Italia!*

SLEEP WRITING AND
STAR WATCHING

At a big social gathering, I meet the mother of an old friend who is dressed
in a white sari like women in the Bible. She talks with me about *Apricot Eggs*,
my fish-life story that made her sad.

Later I travel into the desert with an old girlfriend, with whom I traveled often
in the Mother Lode when we were young. We follow a black road through
endless yellow sand to several withered towns. Finally we come to the sea.

Beneath a wavelike cliff fringed in gold, I begin to sleep write in the sand,
phrases for the night sky. From my position beneath the cliff, I see my husband
pass ghostlike along the dune. He looks up. High above us float a pair
of constellations that move through darkness like swimmers.

Awed by their watery twinkling, I remember the bushwomen in the Kalahari
who raise their babies to the stars to give them sky-magic
before they walk on earth.

Follow the star
Seen from afar.

ARE WE
WHERE WE
REALLY SEE
ALL WE REALLY
ARE

KMN

Sleys Writing   December 28, 1984

Passport to Spring   January 14, 1985

PASSPORT TO SPRING

White fingers in the sky. Slush melts along the road. A sloping snowfield, stretching toward the base of the peaks, is covered with tiny yellow lilies. Wild trillium—a sign of spring, so delicately overwhelming, I forget where I'm going. Mysteries of contrast and continual renewal.

OPEN BOOK

Confusion, changing rooms, fragmented conversations. In the midst of it all,
my potter friend sits down with a small, black, three-holed binder like my
dream book. She opens to a dream whose right side is neatly typed out and
whose left is a fabulous flowing mirage of color.

The Open Book

Confusion, changing
rooms, fragmented
conversations.
In the midst of it...
she opens to a
dream.
The right side is
neatly typed out,
the left a fabulous,
flowing color
image.

February 9, 1985

Sunlight streams through pillars
with a rhythm that is musical,
delicate and ordered in its
progression
is built for sun and shadow
harmonious days and nights, and
the circle of earth, grander by far
than the encircling arms of the
"mother church"

KM

FROM ART CLASS
TO ST. PETER'S

With hands smeared in charcoal dust, I work on a still-life in art class.
The teacher reworks my drawing, adding a right hand in the lower corner.
He tells me to clarify it by erasing black with my kneaded eraser.
What remains reminds me of Redon's lithograph, *The Haunted House*.
White fingers reach through darkness to take hold of a piece of white paper.

On the studio wall, I see the college schedule.
My art appreciation class is not listed.

My journey leads elsewhere, to the palace of the Legion of Honor where
I search for my daughter as she used to be at five or six years old.
When I find her, the museum becomes a ballet. Dancers move
through room after room of pictures, following the ebb and flow
of art history from ancient times to modern.

Outside, the rectangular entrance court of the Legion of Honor
changes shape and size to become Bernini's encircling colonnade
in front of St. Peter's. Sunlight streams through pillars in
a musical ordered progression.

BETWEEN SUN AND MOON

It's time to leave Utah. We move back to San Francisco, to the family house
on Broadway, leaving the Salt Lake Valley blanketed in snow beneath gray
storm skies. Winter is nearly over. A season changes and a life.

At a family celebration, brunch is served by our old French nurse. After the
meal, I enter another celebration in *terra oscura*. An old man takes me down into
earth, along a long, narrow passage that reminds me vaguely of the descent
into the royal tombs in the Valley of Kings. Fear turns to tender
friendship as I take his hand in mine, kiss it softly, and say,
"I'm glad we've been together. We're friends now."

In return and in remembrance of all we've shared, he shows me two
paired statues. One is of green jade, the other of gray stone. The jade pair
he must keep in the heart of earth. The gray pair he gives me.

The jade couple lie face to face on their bellies. Where they touch,
they form a human bridge, like ancient river gods. Together, as male and
female, they make the river flow.

The couple in gray stone repeats this pairing in a vertical position.
The woman crouches down, her mouth almost touching the erect penis of
her consort, who wears the headdress of a pre-Columbian sun god.
In this position, with her behind arched in air, she becomes moon beneath
the crown of sun. Round and round, they join and separate in rhythmic order.

Between Sun and Moon

March 6, 1985

In the midst of this openess is a spring of golden …brook

March 18, 1

HYDRA BEADS

Silence and space. In openness around me a string of gold beads appears
like a necklace that is coming unstrung. Starting out close together,
the beads begin to separate into an arc that looks like the constellation
Hydra—a body of seven stars stretched between Leo and Virgo. The lion
wants to be seen in the world; the lady wants to play in solitude.

SUNSHIELD

Interior walls have been remodeled to allow freer flow of space inside.
Sunlight. Hardwood floors. Richly patterned oriental carpets.

All our comings and goings seem inconsequential to the painted sun,
centered high above large double doors. Shrouded in a bluish cloud, partly
covered by a passing planet, it has been there so long, it is part of the barn.
Slowly, wind, water, and light have softened it, until it shines gently
behind the red planet.

Yellow fades to white.
Red remains.

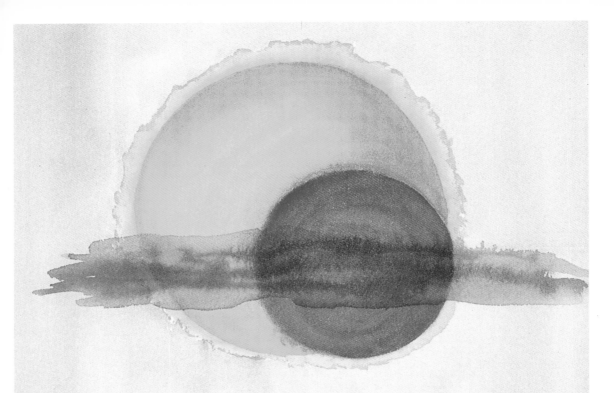

Centered high above
Forever slightly shrouded
A combination of sun,
    and earth and wind
In front floats a red planet,
enwrapped in fast
                moving cloud

April 9, 1985

Words

May 25, 1985

phrases ___ finished
about ___

about words
And a necklace of dreams

In the beginning ___ the ___
Now there is the ___

Hard to ___
Easy to ___

WORD QUILT

Out of conversation and movement through crowded rooms comes
a hybrid vision of thought and feeling that fills my interior.

A reddish patchwork made up of small compartments is stitched together
around a central opening. I think of crazy quilts, scraps of fabric from
many sources, many places, many lives, all pieced together.

Only partially exposed, its lower half is covered by a piece of binder paper
on which are written phrases to be finished. Slide lists and printed
formalities of my curriculum vitae come to mind and pass away. This is not
a typed-up resume, but my handwritten script, which is only half written.

PARIS-LONDON LINE

On a fast-moving train from Paris to London.

Paris: Notre Dame on the Île de la Cité, Louvre, Tuileries, city of love in
daylight as well as dark—Gothic architecture dissolved in light.

London: seat of a political, not a spiritual queen. The National Gallery,
bands in the park, bankers in black bowler hats. Parliament and pubs.
Law and order with an underside of rock 'n' roll.

As our train speeds on, several passengers remark on the good connection we
have. Opposite me is seated an English undertaker with whom I chat politely.
When we come to the French/English border, his whole personality changes as
we enter his native countryside. Riding along the bay, he begins to speak with
deep feeling about the cove beyond the bend where he worked in a hospital as
a boy. Hospital cove. I, too, am excited by the name that recalls the Marin
shore and Angel Island in San Francisco Bay, where I explored and fished as a
child, long before Hospital Cove became a state park packed with tourists.

As we come into the bay, a young boy stands knee deep in the cold British sea.
In his hand he holds a paintbrush dipped in red with which he encircles a small
blue-and-white fishing boat to paint on a new waterline. His tedious repair job
is almost finished. The boat is ready to sail.

When the train stops, the Englishman and I take off our shoes to walk the
beach barefooted together. The pace and space of this shore walk fills me with
life, in contrast to the rapid transit of the train that rushes headlong
down the line, on schedule from city to city.

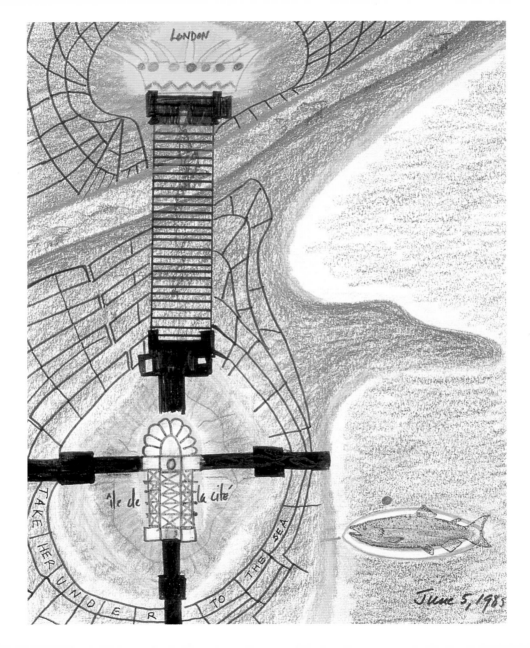

Fish Remains

KMN.   9/18/85

FISH REMAINS

On the morning of my forty-fifth birthday, I enter a gathering of women
who fill a room for an initiation ceremony.

As I walk in, one says, "Strip down to yourself. Take off your dress and iron it
out before you hang it up." I remember the sisters of the shield in *Jaguar Woman*,
the circle of women who took off their masks for the initiate to see inside.

In the middle sits an ironing board piled with clothes. On top of the pile, I pile
my own, and a woman asks me, "Where do you want to begin?"

"Where I end, with a dream."

Menstrual blood stains my aqua nightgown and my bare hands. I go downstairs
to the toilet to clean up before I climb up a long flight of stairs into the basilica
of San Pietro. Before me, under Michelangelo's dome, is a rectangular altar
table of dark stone on which sits a white oval platter shaped like an eye.
On the platter are the remains of pieces of pink fish flesh
that I have chewed and spit out.

I motion to my thirteen-year-old daughter, saying, "This is the bier of
St. Peter." As I speak, a whole fish appears in place of pieces: a darkly
glistening, green-gold steelhead with a full apricot-colored belly.

Reverently, I pick up the platter. We descend the stairs, circle the great sunlit
circle of the colonnade, and return. Inside, I place my offering on the altar in
the middle of the great fishbowl in the center of the Holy See.

YOUR DREAM JOURNAL

The following pages are left blank
for you to begin your own conversation with dreams.
However you catch them, they will release you.
Buona notte e sogni d'oro . . .
. . . good night and golden dreams.

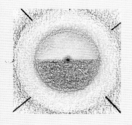